BATS on PARADE

BATS ON PARADE

by Kathi Appelt

illustrated by Melissa Sweet

Morrow Junior Books
New York

To Max the Marvelous, with love
—K.A.

To Barbara, with many thanks
—M.S.

Watercolors, pen and ink, and colored pencils were used for the full-color illustrations.
The text type is 14-point Eras Demi.

Published by Morrow Junior Books
a division of William Morrow and Company, Inc.
1350 Avenue of the Americas, New York, NY 10019
www.williammorrow.com

Printed in Singapore at Tien Wah Press.

10 9 8 7 6 5 4 3 2 1

Library of Congress Cataloging-in-Publication Data
Appelt, Kathi.
Bats on parade/Kathi Appelt; illustrated by Melissa Sweet.
p. cm.
Summary: On a midsummer night the Marching Bat Band makes a rare appearance, its members grouped in formations that demonstrate multiplication from two times two up to ten times ten.
ISBN 0-688-15665-7 (trade)—ISBN 0-688-15666-5 (library)
[1. Bats—Fiction.   2. Marching bands—Fiction.   3. Bands (Music)—Fiction.   4. Multiplication—Fiction.   5. Stories in rhyme.]
I. Sweet, Melissa, ill.   II. Title.   PZ8.3.A554Bau 1999   [E]—dc21   98-23603   CIP   AC

The grandstands were packed
on that midsummer eve,
wing to wing, paw to paw,
beak to beak, sleeve to sleeve.

"Let the good times begin,"
the grand marshal cried,
and a bevy of bats
dropped out of the sky.

There were bats from New Orleans
and bats from Detroit.
There were bats from El Paso
and bats from West Point.

They fluttered and flew
down the Grand Promenade
in a fabulous fanfare
of bats on parade.

The bat rangerettes
did their high-kick routine,
and right behind them
came the bat parade queen.

She waved to the crowd
from her flowery seat,
then floated along
the confetti-strewn street.

The whole exposition
could have stopped when she passed,
but ooohhh noo...
the show wasn't over,
the best was the last.

The air fairly crackled
with anticipation
as the Marching Bat Band
made a rare visitation.

The battalion was led
by **1** drum majorette
who blew her shrill whistle
and off they were set.

1x1=1

First stepped the piccolos
piping in twos.

There were 4 of those pipers
with spats on their shoes.

2x2=4

Next came the flute players
all in a line.
They marched three by three—
9
which comes out to **9** .

3 X 3 = 9

16 in the regiment played clarinets. In four sets of four came those classy cadets.

4x4=16

Up marched the saxophones,
all **25**—
sopranos and altos,
they came five by five.

5 x 5 = 25

Bat-a-tat, bat-a-tat
boomed the wild rhythm section.

What a proud **36**!
What a drum corps collection!

Snare drums and bass drums,
marimbas and cymbals—
six sets of sixes—
triangles and timbals.

6×6=36

And right on their heels,
their golden horns gleaming,

49 trumpets
in sevens came streaming.

7 x 7 = 49

Count them: **64** French horns,
their brassy bells raised,
by eights they advanced
down the Grand Promenade.

And just when the crowd
thought it couldn't get better,
the trombones arrived—

81 altogether.

In nine rows of nine
those trombones reported,
while there, right behind them,
the tubas retorted.

The crowd was bedazzled
at what they saw then—

100 sousaphones marched
ten by ten.

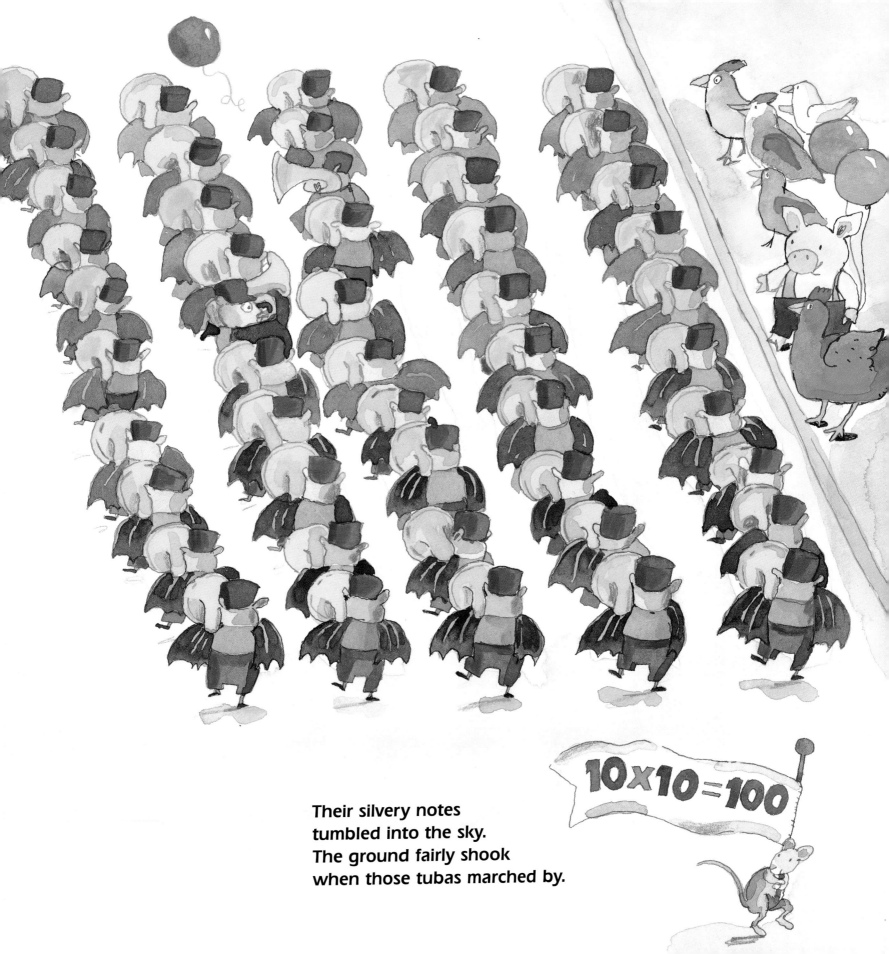

Their silvery notes
tumbled into the sky.
The ground fairly shook
when those tubas marched by.

10×10=100

The crowd was ecstatic.
They hooted, they hopped,
as the drum majorette
blew the whistle to stop.

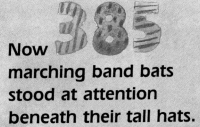

Now **385**
marching band bats
stood at attention
beneath their tall hats.

They turned toward the grandstand.
What flourish! What flair!
Then that old "Stars and Stripes"
filled the midsummer air.

Their instruments gleamed
in the light of the stars
as that tuneful battalion
played their last bars.

Then 385
bats in that crew
saluted the crowd
as up they all flew.

Oh, never was seen
a more wonderful sight
than the Marching Bat Band
on that midsummer night!